Lee Canter's

Help! It's Homework Time

Improving Your Child's Homework Habits

By Lee Canter and
Marlene Canter

Lee Canter's Effective Parenting Books

Editorial Staff
Barbara Schadlow
Marcia Shank
Bob Winberry
Kathy Winberry

Book Design
Bob Winberry

Cover Illustration
Patty Briles

P.O. Box 2113, Santa Monica, CA 90407-2113
800-262-4347 310-395-3221

Printed in the United States of America
First printing December 1993

99 98 97 96 95 10 9 8 7 6 5 4 3

ISBN 0-939007-75-4

Parents Want to Know

Questions & Answers 6

Homework Help Is on the Way!

The 5-Step Homework Plan 9

Step 1 - Schedule Daily Homework Time 10

Step 2 - Set Up a Study Area 13

Step 3 - Create a Homework Survival Kit 15

Step 4 - Let Your Child Know How Important Homework Is 18

Step 5 - Praise Your Child 20

Long-Range Planning

Help with Written Reports, Science Projects and More 22

Solving the Most Common Homework Problems 23

Should I Call the Teacher? 27

If Problems Persist 28

How to Speak So Your Child Will Listen 31

Homework Worksheets

Planning Sheets, Awards and More 35

Top 10 Homework Reminders 47

Homework
—and the nightly battles!

Mom, Jason keeps bugging me while I'm studying for my test.

But that's not the way the teacher taught us to do that!

"Do we have any colored pencils? I've got to make a map of Canada tonight."

"Let me watch one more TV show and then I'll do my homework."

I don't have any homework tonight. I already did it at school.

Sound familiar?

Packed alongside every assignment brought home from school is a bundle of questions, confusion and negative feelings—enough to cause a nightly battle between you and your child. This doesn't need to be the case.

All children argue with their parents about homework from time to time, but when battles over homework become routine, it's time to take action.

Parents Want to Know
Questions & Answers

You want the best for your child and that means you want your child to succeed in school. Homework is an important part of that success. Why then is homework so exasperating? Why does homework lead to so many frustrating and exhausting nights of confusion?

Here are questions other parents have asked expressing these same concerns.

Q I would like to help my daughter with her homework, but we end up fighting instead.

ANSWER: When you work with your daughter, make it clear to her that you are only dealing with homework. Other issues, such as discipline concerns that may have developed during the day or week before, are not to be discussed or brought up during homework time. Explain to her that you are here now to help with homework and any hurt feelings should be put aside for awhile. During homework time, it's a good time to bury the hatchet.

Q Is there any way I can help my child with a book report that's not due for a couple of weeks?

ANSWER: Learning how to plan out projects that extend over a period of time is no simple matter. In order to reach such long-range goals, one must have a long-range plan. By using a Long-Range Planner (page 36), you will help your child understand how to break up a project into smaller, easier to accomplish tasks.

Q My son insists that he never has any homework, that he's completed it all at school.

ANSWER: First, ask him to bring his assignments home so you can look over them. Explain that you expect him to show you every night: 1) the assignments given by his teachers and 2) the work he's done. If the assignments involve reading, ask him to show you the book and offer to give a spot quiz. If your child says he's left all his books and work at school, insist that he bring his books home every night—whether he has homework or not. See page 24 for more details.

Q My daughter does such sloppy work that I can hardly make sense of it. Are there any solutions to a child's poor study habits?

ANSWER: Sloppy work can come from two sources: 1) no appropriate study area, 2) there is little respect or motivation for what one is doing. By establishing a study area (page 13), your daughter will tackle the first problem. In order to tackle the second, it might help to communicate to your daughter the importance of homework (page 18), and to clearly state your expectations.

Q My daughter is eleven years old and every morning it's still the same old thing—a frantic search for homework, books and anything else that needs to go to school. Too often completed assignments get left behind and signed notes never make it back to the classroom.

ANSWER: A Homework Drop Spot can solve this problem. A Homework Drop Spot is a location in the home where everything that needs to go back to school the next day is deposited—the night before. Having a "drop spot" will help your child develop the habit of always putting completed assignments in the same place each night.

Q I work evenings, so it's difficult for me to control when my kids do their homework. Any suggestions?

ANSWER: It's difficult for many parents to be home when it's time for their children to do their homework. First, schedule Daily Homework Time (page 10) and insist that homework be done during that time. You might try monitoring your child's homework habits by making a call just before this homework time is to begin. If you are unable to call, have your child leave his work in a certain spot so you can go over it when you do get home to be sure that the work is getting done.

Q I let my child listen to the radio when she does her homework. She says it helps her to concentrate. Is this OK?

ANSWER: For most children, listening to the radio, though calming and comforting at first, tends to lead to distraction after a while. Your daughter may find the radio relaxing, but in the long haul, she will be much better off learning to work in a quiet environment with no distractions.

Q My daughter is juggling a heavy academic load, extracurricular activities and family obligations. Is there any way I can help her to manage all these activities?

ANSWER: Yes, try the Daily Schedule on page 39. Time management is a great concept to learn at a young age. By having your daughter work with a Daily Schedule, she will see how to avoid overlapping activities and avoid over scheduling. Taking control of one's time is a skill that, once a habit, can lead to a more productive and less frustrating school life.

Q My son is struggling with math and I am considering getting a tutor for him. Any thoughts?

ANSWER: Before you bring in a tutor, check to see that you've made doing homework as productive as possible for your son. Have you set up a study area (see page 13)? Is it quiet? Are their supplies nearby so your son can do his work without interruptions (see page 15)? Has a Daily Homework Time been set up so that your son can concentrate on his assignments without worrying about missing his sports practice or other responsibilities (see page 10)? If you've helped your child to this point, and he continues to struggle with his assignments, a tutor is an excellent idea. Talk to your child's teacher first. Many teachers have students in class that they assign to be peer tutors.

Homework Help

is on the way!

If homework is an ongoing hassle in your home you're not alone. It's the cause of nightly battles, tears and frustration for many parents. At the end of a busy day the last thing parents want to do is fight with their child over a book report due the next day, a page of math problems or seemingly endless worksheets filled with social studies questions.

Like their children, parents often wish homework would disappear altogether.

How do you improve the situation?

Start by changing your own perception of homework. When you recognize how important homework is for your child, you'll be more motivated to follow through with the steps you need to take to help your child with homework.

First, take a look at these homework pluses:

☆ Students who consistently do homework perform better academically than those who do not do homework.

☆ By doing homework, students can improve academic achievement in all subjects.

☆ Aside from teaching academic lessons, homework teaches a child to:

- follow directions.
- start and complete work on time.
- learn to be responsible.
- be self-reliant.

Homework Builds Responsibility

For many children, homework is the first time they have a responsibility all their own. It's up to them to bring it home. It's up to them to do the work. And it's up to them to see that the work gets back to school. From the moment the teacher gives the assignment to the moment it is turned in, the responsibility rests on your child's shoulders.

The responsible habits a child learns through homework will effect his or her success not only in school, but later in the workplace.

Homework has some pluses for you, too!

Homework is a unique opportunity for you to share in your child's education, personal growth and future. It's a chance to participate on a daily basis—to let your child know through your interest and concern that you believe in his or her potential. A child's school years are fleeting—and in reality the chances you have to shape his educational experience are limited.

Make the most of homework, and help your child make the most of his or her school years.

The goal of this book is to give you the resources you need to turn homework from a nightly battle to nightly success. We begin by following the 5-Step Homework Plan.

The 5-Step Homework Plan

The foundation of your efforts will be the 5-Step Homework Plan. Let's take a look at each step now:

STEP 1
Schedule Daily Homework Time.
Your child should have a specific time each day to do homework. You'll learn how to plan Daily Homework Time, how to put it into action, and how to make it work.

STEP 2
Set Up a Study Area.
Nobody can do their best work in the middle of family commotion. Your child needs a quiet place in which to study. A designated study area lets your child know that you place a priority on homework, and care enough to make sure there's a place in which to do it.

STEP 3
Create a Homework Survival Kit.
Does your child always have the supplies on hand that he or she needs to do assignments? Or is the great "pen and paper search" part of your nightly homework battle? The Homework Survival Kit will bring a peaceful resolution to this recurring problem.

STEP 4
Talk to Your Child about the Importance of Homework.
When homework has been an ongoing battle, it's easy for everyone to feel negatively about it. Your child has likely had a few choice comments to share on the subject, and chances are you've made some less-than-complimentary pronouncements yourself. *Enough!* Once you commit yourself to turning homework from nightmare to success, you need to take a more positive, assertive stance. Your child needs to understand the importance you place on homework. Your words and your actions must communicate this message.

In Step 4 you'll learn the words that work and the actions that get results.

STEP 5
Praise Your Child.
It's easy to criticize your child when homework isn't done. It's a lot harder to remember to give applause for assignments completed. It's important to remember that your words of praise, more than anything else, will motivate your child to do his or her best work. Tips and reminders included here will help you keep praiseworthy comments on the tip of your tongue.

STEP 1 Helping with Homework

Schedule Daily Homework Time.

Does your child seem to have time for everything *but* homework? Somehow there always seems to be enough hours in the day for sports, TV, friends or other activities, but when it comes to getting homework done, time just runs out. The result? Those familiar late-night battles, tears, and children who are too tired to do their best work anyway.

It's your child's responsibility to do homework, but it's your responsibility to see to it that he or she does it. One way you can help your child meet this responsibility and develop good study habits is to schedule Daily Homework Time.

What is Daily Homework Time?

Daily Homework Time is a preplanned time set aside each day during which your child must do homework. During Daily Homework Time all other activities must stop. Your child must go to his or her study area and get to work.

Here's how to schedule Daily Homework Time:

1. Sit with your child and discuss how much time is needed each day for homework. Younger children may only need a half-hour; older children might need one and a half to two hours each night.
2. Using the Daily Schedule sheet (page 39), help your child fill in his or her scheduled activities for the week including any after-school activities (sports, practice, music lessons, etc.) and responsibilities (babysitting, chores at home, etc.) in the spaces provided. If appropriate, you might ask your child to choose one favorite TV program each night and mark that space as well.
3. Now, look at the spaces that are left unfilled. Which of these would be the best time each day for your child to do homework? Have your child fill in the spaces which will be designated Daily Homework Time for each day of the week.
4. Check your child's schedule for accuracy and appropriateness, and then hang the Daily Schedule up in a prominent location.

Encourage your child to stick to the schedule. Once your child gets the idea, he or she will be able to update the Daily Schedule as needed, week by week.

First, your child fills in his or her scheduled activities for the week.

Next, he or she chooses the best time each day for Daily Homework Time.

Daily SCHEDULE

MONDAY
3:00 PM Scouts
4:00 PM
5:00 PM
6:00 PM Dinner
Homework Time: 7:00 to 8:00
7:00 PM Homework
8:00 PM
9:00 PM
10:00 PM

TUESDAY
3:00 PM Babysit
4:00 PM Homework
5:00 PM
6:00 PM Dinner
Homework Time: 4:00 to 5:00
7:00 PM
8:00 PM
9:00 PM
10:00 PM

WEDNESDAY
3:00 PM Softball Practice
4:00 PM
5:00 PM
6:00 PM Dinner
Homework Time: 7:00 to 8:00
7:00 PM Homework
8:00 PM
9:00 PM
10:00 PM

THURSDAY
3:00 PM Homework
4:00 PM
5:00 PM Babysit
6:00 PM Dinner
Homework Time: 3:00 to 4:00
7:00 PM
8:00 PM
9:00 PM
10:00 PM

FRIDAY
3:00 PM No Homework!
4:00 PM
5:00 PM
6:00 PM
Homework Time: to
7:00 PM
8:00 PM
9:00 PM
10:00 PM

Explain to your child why Daily Homework Time is important.

"One reason you don't always get homework done is because you never seem to have time to do it. To help solve this problem we're going to schedule Daily Homework Time. During Daily Homework Time I expect you to stop everything else and complete your homework assignments. No more putting it off until later—every day you'll know exactly when you're going to do homework."

When Daily Homework Time is scheduled, you and your child will both know when homework is to be done. No more arguing about when to do homework. No more putting homework off until the last minute. This will free you from conflict in the evening as well as ensure that time has been set aside for your child's schoolwork.

Making Daily Homework Time Work

Just scheduling Daily Homework Time may not be enough to change your child's homework habits. If you want to guide your child toward more consistently *responsible* habits, you'll need to stay involved.

Here are some ideas to keep Daily Homework Time working:

1 Check to see that your child starts homework on time.
If your child is younger, you may need to remind him or her when Daily Homework Time begins. Older children will learn to be responsible for watching the clock themselves. Once Daily Homework Time has begun give it a few minutes, then drop in and see that homework is underway.

2 Check to see that your child finishes all work during Daily Homework Time.
As Daily Homework Time comes to a close, it's a good idea to take another quick look at your child's work. Are the assignments complete? Neatly done? If yes, give your child a hug and words of praise. If no, talk with your child to find out what the problem was and how it can be corrected.

When you care enough to check on your child's progress, you are telling your child how important it is to do homework—and that you care about homework even if you can't be home during homework time.

When you can't be home during Daily Homework Time

Today more than ever, many children must schedule their Daily Homework Time when no parent is home. This doesn't have to be a problem.

- If you are able to, give your child a call from work at the start of Daily Homework Time. You can find out if your child is doing homework and give a welcomed hello at the same time. Also, you can clear away any small roadblocks your child might perceive to be in the way (i.e., siblings being noisy, can't find a book, etc.).
- If you can't call, have your child leave homework out for you to look at when you do get home. If the work is completed, you'll know that your child was getting his or her work done.

Help for Speeders and Forgetters!

Does your child speed through assignments, resulting in messy, incomplete work? Or does your child forget to bring assignments home altogether? Required Homework Time may be the answer you've been looking for! Required Homework Time means that your child must use the entire scheduled Daily Homework Time for homework or other academic activities such as reading whether homework is brought home or not, whether homework is completed or not. For example, if one hour is allotted each night for homework, then that hour must be used for "scholarly" pursuits one way or another. Required Homework Time teaches your child that there is no advantage to forgetting homework or speeding through assignments.

STEP 2

Helping with Homework

Set Up a Study Area.

Picture this: A child is settled in front of the TV with food to the left and sodas to the right. The radio is blaring, the dog is licking up crumbs off the carpet, little brother and sister are playing tag around the sofa. The child turns and says, "I don't understand this problem."

You wonder to yourself, which problem?

To do homework successfully, your child must have a proper place in which to work and have all necessary supplies close at hand.

Here's what to do:

Choose a spot in your home to be your child's study area.
Work with your child and choose a good place to call a study area. It doesn't need to be a lot of space, it just needs to be well-lit, comfortable and quiet during home-work time. The kitchen table or a corner of the living room is fine.

Set aside this area during Daily Homework Time.
When choosing this area, make sure it will be quiet during Daily Homework Time. Whenever possible, keep the study area off limits to brothers and sisters during this time.

Turn off the radio and TV in the study area during Daily Homework Time.
Though many children prefer it, the TV and radio should not be playing when homework is being done. If brothers and sisters are around, have them do their activities in another room. If that's not possible, you must simply insist that during Daily Homework Time the TV remains off.

Personalize the study area!
When your child feels a sense of pride and ownership about his or her study area, that sense of pride may carry over into homework. Encourage your child to hang a sign labeling the area as his or her study space. Placing a favorite picture or placemat in the area is also a nice idea.

Explain to your child why it's important to do homework in a study area.

"It's important for you to concentrate and be able to think when you do your homework. That's hard to do if there are lots of noises and distractions. I want you to do your best work, and that's why I want you to always do your homework in your study area. I'll help make sure that you won't be disturbed. You can do your part by always going to your study area during Daily Homework Time, and staying there until your homework is done."

More Study Area Guidelines

Grades K-3

Choose the study area *with* your child. This is a good opportunity to talk about why one place may be better than another. Is it quiet enough here? Do you have enough room? Can you see in this light? Make sure the location you choose is near to you so that you can be available for help if it's needed.

Grades 4-6

Guide your child in choosing an appropriate location, but give him or her a chance to do some independent decision making. Talk together about which places in your home might be better than others for doing homework. Children this age often like to plop on the floor or bed to do their work. This may be fine for reading, but encourage your child to do written work at a desk or table.

Grades 7 and up

Your child should choose his own study area, but you need to make sure it is in an appropriate location. Music and TV are favorite teenage pastimes during homework time, but stay firm. Your child will do better work in a quiet environment.

Do Not Disturb!

Every time your child is interrupted it takes two to three minutes to regain concentration. That's a lot of wasted time, and that's one of the reasons homework seems to stretch into eternity some nights. Homework time must be respected—by all family members. Some families find that a "Do Not Disturb" sign is a great way to alert everyone that it's study time. Give your child the "Do Not Disturb" sign on page 37—a timely reminder to hang up when it's time to work. The "Homework Is Fun—After It's Done!" poster on the back can help decorate your child's study area.

STEP

3 Helping with Homework

Create a Homework Survival Kit

Once your child begins homework you don't want him or her wasting time searching the house for a pair of scissors, tape, pencils or paper—or anything else that might be needed to complete assignments.

An important key to getting homework done is having supplies in one place. A Homework Survival Kit, containing supplies needed to do homework—will prevent your child from being continually distracted by the need to go searching for supplies, and will free you from last minute trips to the store for must-have but don't-have items.

On the following pages you will find sample Homework Survival Kit supply lists for different age groups. Take a look at the list appropriate for your child.

Here's how to put together your Homework Survival Kit:

First, find a container.
A shoe box, an old lunch box, a hat box, or anything that can hold all of the items listed for your child's grade level will do as a container for the Homework Survival Kit. If your child would enjoy it, have him or her decorate the box to give it a personal touch.

Next, gather the items.
Check out the appropriate list on the following pages and gather any of the items you might have already. (Mark those off the list). Then take the list with you to the store and buy the additional items. Most of these items can be found at your local toy store, teacher's supply store or the corner drug store.

Finally, keep the Homework Survival Kit nearby.
Your Homework Survival Kit should be kept near the study area, ready to reach when needed. Your Homework Survival Kit won't hold *everything* your child might need for every assignment, but it will be there for the majority of homework needs.

Respect your child's Homework Survival Kit. Don't use these supplies for other family needs. Providing your child with important homework supplies will help your child do his or her best work.

Homework Survival Kit
SUPPLIES Grades K-3

- [ ] crayons*
- [ ] pencils*
- [ ] erasers*
- [ ] writing paper*
- [ ] scissors*
- [ ] pencil sharpener
- [ ] glue or paste
- [ ] pens
- [ ] tape
- [ ] markers
- [ ] construction paper
- [ ] hole punch
- [ ] stapler
- [ ] children's dictionary
- [ ] paper clips
- [ ] ruler
- [ ] rubber bands
- [ ] drawing paper

* These are the most important supplies your child needs. Try to obtain these items as soon as possible. Add additional supplies as you are able to.

Homework Survival Kit
SUPPLIES Grades 4-6

- [ ] pencils*
- [ ] pens*
- [ ] erasers*
- [ ] writing paper*
- [ ] scissors*
- [ ] markers
- [ ] pencil sharpener
- [ ] drawing paper
- [ ] tape
- [ ] colored pencils
- [ ] construction paper
- [ ] hole punch
- [ ] stapler
- [ ] paper clips
- [ ] glue or paste
- [ ] folder for reports
- [ ] index cards
- [ ] thesaurus
- [ ] intermediate dictionary
- [ ] assignment book

Homework Survival Kit
SUPPLIES Grades 7-12

- ☐ assignment book*
- ☐ pencils*
- ☐ pens*
- ☐ writing paper*
- ☐ erasers*
- ☐ whiteout
- ☐ markers
- ☐ tape
- ☐ hole punch
- ☐ pencil sharpener
- ☐ scissors
- ☐ ruler
- ☐ stapler
- ☐ colored pencils
- ☐ paper clips
- ☐ index cards
- ☐ dictionary
- ☐ compass
- ☐ protractor
- ☐ thesaurus

Explain why the Homework Survival Kit is an important part of getting homework done.

"How do you feel when you have to spend homework time looking for pencils, paper or anything else you need? It's a waste of time, and frustrating, isn't it? To help solve this problem we're going to put together a box filled with all the supplies you need to do homework. We'll call this a Homework Survival Kit, and we'll keep it in your study area. I'll help you put it together, but you'll have to do your part by using these supplies just for homework, and letting me know when anything is running out."

STEP 4 Help with Homework

Let Your Child Know How Important Homework Is

Don't underestimate the influence you have on your child. Your words can and do make a difference in how your child approaches responsibilities. If you communicate ambivalence about homework—

"Fine, go to bed. I'm sure the teacher won't mind a missed assignment here and there"

or even negativity

"I wouldn't do this assignment either. Does your teacher think we have nothing else to do at night?"

—your child can't be blamed for feeling the same way.

Let your child know that homework is important.

What you say and how you say it will go a long way in emphasizing the importance *you* place on education—which will directly effect the importance your child will place on homework.

Sit with your child and speak calmly and firmly:

"Homework is just as important as the work you do in school every day. I care about you, and I want you to do your best."

When children are very young, adults make all their decisions for them. Adults structure their activities, plan their meals and put them to bed. As children grow, adults guide them into making choices of their own while keeping a close eye on which choices they make.

Homework is an excellent opportunity to see to it that your child makes the right choices about academic success.

Actions can speak louder than words.

It's important to *tell* your child exactly what you expect regarding homework. It's just as important to consistently *show* your child how you feel.

Here are some things you can do to let your child know that when it comes to homework, you're going to stay involved:

• Ask each night to see your child's completed homework.

You probably make every effort to pay attention to your child's sports events, recitals or anything else he or she works hard at. Homework takes a lot of effort, too, and children want that effort to be noticed and appreciated. Asking to see your child's completed work gives you an opportunity to give it a quick appraisal, but most important it gives you an opportunity to praise your child's hard work.

• Respect your child's study area and homework supplies.

Don't sabotage your homework plan! Resist the ever-present temptation to borrow a colored marker (*I'll put it back later*) from the Homework Survival Kit or turn on the TV (*real low*). The example you set *is* an important part of your homework message.

• Check your child's assignment book or homework sheet each night. This is the best way to keep on top of your child's homework and stay informed about what's going on in class. Checking your child's list of assignments should be part of your own nightly routine—one that your child learns to expect. Younger children often need a reminding nudge to make sure everything gets done, and older children are often given assignments on Monday that are due later in the week. By checking the assignment sheet, you can help your child stay on track.

If your child's teacher does not provide or require assignment sheets or books, by all means provide one for your child and insist that it be used.

You can make sheets yourself or purchase one of the many commercial assignment books that are available.

• Ask about any long-range assignments that may be upcoming. Children often need help organizing and planning their written reports and science projects. Trips to the library and gathering needed materials take time (yours as well as your child's). The sooner you are informed about about these long-range projects, the better you can help your child stay on top of them. (See page 22 for specific tips on helping your child with long-range projects.)

If you have any questions or concerns talk to your child's teacher.

You wouldn't hesitate to call your doctor if you were concerned about your child's health. Your concerns about your child's education are every bit as important—and your child's teacher is the professional who is ready to help you.

STEP Helping with Homework

5 Praise your child.

The single most important step you can take to encourage your child to do homework is to give praise—and lots of it. Praise lets your child feel good about what he or she is doing. Good feelings bring about good work.

• Consistently praise your child's homework efforts.

Don't save your praise for days when a 100% test comes home. Praise your child for his or her efforts daily. Let your child know that you appreciate just how well he or she is working and that the effort shows.

• Praise your child about specific accomplishments.

When your child shows you his or her work, take a look at it and respond to some specific point.

"Nine out of ten questions correct. That's excellent! Great job, Cindy!"

sounds a lot more sincere than simply,

"Great job!"

Paying attention to the efforts your child is giving towards homework lets your child know that you really do care.

Try a Little Super Praise!

Super praise is a powerful way to let your child know how proud you are of his or her efforts. Here's how to use it:

First, one parent praises the child:

"You did a great job finishing all of your homework during Daily Homework Time. I'll make sure Dad hears about this when he gets home."

Second, this parent praises the child in front of the other parent:

"Bob did a really fine job on his homework today. He started it on time and stayed with it until it was done."

Finally, the other parent praises the child:

"Bob, I'm really proud of you, getting such a good report from Mom. You're doing a terrific job! Keep it up!"

If you're a single parent, use a grandparent, neighbor, or a family friend as your partner in delivering Super Praise. Any adult whose approval your child will value can fill the role of the second person offering praise.

All children, from kindergarten through high school, need and want their parents' words of recognition. Get into the habit of praising your children often. You'll be pleasantly surprised to see how positive praise can be!

Homework TRACKER

Week of:	Monday	Tuesday	Wednesday	Thursday	Friday
to					
to					
to					
to					

Use this sheet to keep track of completed homework. Check off one square each night that all homework is completed.

HOMEWORK COUPON

Outstanding Planning!

Here's something special just for you!

Homework Tracker

Here's an easy way to keep track of completed homework assignments and reward your child for a job well done. Remove the Homework Trackers on page 41. Review your child's work and then check off one square each night homework is completed neatly and on time. When a specific number of checks have been accumulated, your child receives something special from you.

Tell your child:

> "Each time you complete your homework during Daily Homework Time, I'll check off one square. When you have 5 checks, you'll earn a special reward."

Homework Headliners

What happens to homework once it's checked by the teacher and returned to your child? Give returned homework assignments a little positive exposure. Ask your child to choose work he or she is proud of to be displayed on the refrigerator or a wall. Add a little extra fun by adding stickers or comments of your own to the work. "You're a homework hero, Robert!" "Great work, Julie. I knew you could do it!"

"Homework Hero" Coupons

To show how much you appreciate your child's efforts, give special homework award coupons for specific accomplishments.

Cut out the coupons on pages 43-44 and then fill in a reward such as:

- 1 extra hour of TV,
- friend stays the night,
- special dinner, or
- pick a video.

Give the completed "Homework Hero" coupon to your deserving child!

> "You turned in all your homework this week. Here's a Homework Hero coupon entitling you to pick a video we'll all watch together on Saturday. Good job!"

Each night praise your child about a specific accomplishment.

Long-Range Planning

Help with written reports, science projects and more.

Most homework your child brings home is due the following day or by the end of the week. There are occasions, however, when a long-range project is assigned, and this type of homework needs to be tackled with an "advanced planning" approach.

Long-range projects, such as book reports, term papers, science projects and test preparation, tend to overwhelm school-age children. As a result, these are the assignments that are often put off until the last minute and then cause "panic attacks" for both you and your child.

Relax. Your child doesn't need to panic, and neither do you. With a little planning, long-range projects and papers can turn out to be the most enjoyable assignments of the entire school year—for both you and your child.

That's where the Long-Range Planner comes in handy. By using the Long-Range Planner, your child will learn how to break down a big project into smaller, easy-to-complete tasks, each with it's own "mini deadline" to help keep your child on track.

Four Easy Steps for Long-Range Planning

When your child brings home a long-range project, sit down together for a project planning session and follow the steps below to ensure successful completion of the assignment. Use the Long-Range Planner on pages 35 and 36.

Step 1: Break the assignment down into small parts.
Ask your child to explain to you the teacher's requirements for the project and all the work that will be involved to produce the final product. List all of these requirements and activities on the Long-Range Planner in the sequence they should be done.

Step 2. Set a "mini deadline" for each small part.
With your child, determine a sensible completion date for each activity listed. Have your child write all of these "mini deadlines" on the Long-Range Planner.

Step 3: Schedule time for working on each part.
Help your child stick to a schedule so that each mini deadline can be met. For example, if Step One is "select books on your topic from the library," make sure your child can get to the library. Long-range projects *are* difficult. Your reminders and support will help your child learn how to handle them successfully.

Step 4: Check off each step as it is completed.
Be sure to give plenty of praise for good effort and for achieving each mini goal throughout the course of the project.

Solving the Most Common
Homework Problems

In spite of all the steps you've taken, it isn't uncommon for specific homework problems to still arise. Don't worry. The goal of the following pages is to give you specific solutions to these problems that you can begin using right away. By helping your child solve these problems now you will prevent them from becoming more serious later.

First, Pinpoint the Problem

As you read the problems listed below, check the one(s) that applies to your child.

____A: My child does not do his or her best work.

____B: My child's homework seems difficult to do.

____C: My child fails to bring assignments home.

____D: My child takes all night to finish homework.

____E: My child will not do homework on his or her own.

____F: My child waits until the last minute to finish assignments.

____G: My child will not do homework if I'm not home.

Then, Take Action

Take a look at the suggestions presented. Try the solution that you feel will work with your child.

PROBLEM A: My child does not do his or her best work.

___ a. Often children don't do their best work because they are rushing through homework in order to play, talk on the phone, or watch TV. Take away this incentive by instituting Required Homework Time. Tell your child that he or she must stay in the study area for the *entire* Daily Homework Time. If homework is completed before Daily Homework Time is over, your child must *remain* in the Study Area and *continue to work* until Daily Homework Time is over. For additional information on Required Homework Time see page 12.

___ b. Have your child fill out a Quality Control Checklist. Take a look at your child's work and make a list of those areas that need attention. For example:

Quality Control Checklist

___ I followed all directions.
___ I used my best ideas.
___ I did my work neatly.
___ I checked for mistakes.
___ I corrected my mistakes.
___ I am proud of the work I did.

When your child checks everything off, give him or her lots of praise.

___ c. Ask your child's teacher to send a note home to inform you when a well-done homework assignment is turned in by your child. Share the good news with your child and let him or her know how impressed you and the teacher are with the improvement.

PROBLEM B: My child's homework seems difficult to do.

___ a. Determine whether or not your child is able to do the work. If he or she makes a genuine effort and is still unable to do the work, offer to help. Be careful not to *do* the homework for your child.

___ b. Sometimes children simply need a bit of coaxing. If you've looked your child's work over and are confident she can do it, stand by for a moment or two and give some encouraging words about doing your best work. Perhaps break the assignment down into smaller chunks and offer suggestions on how to complete one or two of these small steps. Then, explain to your child that you have confidence she can do the rest and then leave her alone to do so. At the end of Daily Homework Time, check the work and give praise for work well done.

___ c. If your child still can't do the work even with your help, or if you are unable to help your child with the work, phone or write the teacher. Express your concern about the appropriateness of the assignment for your child's ability. If your teacher is comfortable with the assignment given, ask about a tutor for your child.

PROBLEM C: My child fails to bring assignments home.

___ a. Take away your child's incentive to "forget" homework by insisting on Required Homework Time (see page 12). Your child won't be as likely to leave work at school if he or she knows that time will be spent on academic work whether homework is brought home or not.

___ b. Provide your child with a pocket-size notepad, assignment book or daily calendar. Explain to your child that this book is to be used daily to write down all assignments in all classes. When no assignments are given, they are to write that down also. The key here is that your child learns to make a habit of writing down all daily assignments so you can follow up at home.

___ c. Make sure your child knows that it is his or her responsibility to write down all assignments and to bring the necessary books and papers home to do them. If an assignment *is* forgotten, have your child phone a friend or classmate to get the assignment.

___ d. Tape a note onto your child's binder, or pin a note inside his or her backpack which reads, "Remember homework!" or "Have you forgotten something? (Homework!)".

PROBLEM D: My child takes all night to do homework.

___ a. Go over the Daily Homework Time schedule with your child. Let him or her know that, just as it's important to start homework on time, it's important to finish it on time also. Reward your child with a star for every night that he or she completes homework on time. When your child has received 5 stars, reward this effort with an extra TV show, having a friend stay over, or a special meal.

___ b. Plan a favorite activity for you and your child to do together after homework is completed (bake cookies, play a game, watch a video). Half an hour of one-on-one time with you may be plenty of motivation for your child.

___ c. Have your child do homework in order of difficulty, starting with the hardest assignments first. Saving the easiest for last will help your child gain momentum while working.

___ d. If your child continues to linger through homework, check for distractions. First, look around the study area. Is it well lit? Are there noises coming in from other rooms or the street? If you find any distractions, see if you can eliminate them. Next, talk with your child and ask if there's anything preoccupying his or her mind. Is there something going on at school that's got him or her upset? Finally, if there are no apparent reasons for taking all night to do homework, use a Homework Contract (page 45) or Required Homework Time (page 12).

PROBLEM E: My child won't do homework on his own.

___ a. Give your child 5 to 10 minutes of your undivided attention before Daily Homework Time. Then explain to your child that you both have things to do and that after Daily Homework Time is over, you can both get back together and talk about what you've done.

___ b. Place three pencils on your child's desk. Explain that he must learn to work on his own, and may ask only three questions. For each question asked, you will take a pencil away. If at the end of Daily Homework Time there is at least one pencil left, he may have a reward: extra TV, pick a video for the weekend, bake a cake.

___ c. Anytime you find your child working independently, give praise. Explain that you're very proud that she's learning to be so independent.

___ d. Help your child only after he or she has attempted to do the work on his or her own. Then, only help with small parts of the assignment, just to get your child off and running. Once you see that your child has got the hang of it, let him or her know that you won't be back to help until this particular assignment has been completed.

PROBLEM F: My child waits until the last minute to complete long-term projects (book reports, etc.).

___ a. Ask the teacher for a schedule that shows specific completion dates for when each part of a project should be completed.

___ b. Use the Long-Range Planner (page 35) to write down assignments and completion dates for all parts of the project.

___ c. Go over the project with your child when she first receives it. Help your child understand that in order to do this type of work, she must plan each step and each step must be completed before the next step can start. Work with your child so that an understanding develops that not all homework can be done in one sitting on one night.

___ d. Give your child lots of praise and positive recognition when each step of the project is completed on time. When the whole project is finished, let your child know how proud you are that he was able to tackle such a big assignment.

PROBLEM G: My child won't do work unless I'm there.

___ a. Explain to your child that you will be calling him or her on the phone before, during and after Daily Homework Time. Let your child know that you will be checking in to offer help and motivation, but that these calls will be short and to the point because you both have work to get back to.

___ b. Have your child leave completed homework out for you to check when you get home. This puts him on notice that you will be looking at his assignments and checking to see that they are completed.

___ c. Find a "Study Buddy" for your child, someone he or she can call if help is needed and you're not there—an aunt or uncle, close friend, past babysitter, or any trusted adult who might be willing and able to assist your child when problems arise.

___ d. Offer incentives. Let your child know that if his or her homework is completed when you get home, you can both spend some time together. If homework is not finished, then there will be no quality time together. Other incentives might be that if homework is completed all week long, your child may choose a TV program or video to watch with the family on the weekend.

Should I call the teacher?

Never hesitate to contact your child's teacher if you have a question about homework (or any other school matter). The teacher will welcome your interest. After all, your involvement makes his or her job—helping your child—easier.

These guidelines will help you when it's time to contact your child's teacher.

Contact the teacher if:

• Your child consistently has difficulty doing the homework assignments.
Your child should be able to do assigned work on his own. If he really seems lost, and you know that he has tried, it's time to talk to the teacher.

• Your child consistently does not bring assigned work home.
You can try giving your child Required Homework Time (see page 12) or using a Homework Contract (page 45), but you may wish to unite with the teacher in solving this problem. The teacher can offer incentives at school that may be meaningful to your child. Sometimes a little outside help can do wonders.

• Your child tells you he or she never has homework.
A quick call to the teacher can easily answer this question. Keep in mind also that you have every right to expect to be notified if homework assignments are not being turned in. If your child isn't doing homework, you should know about it.

• Your child says he or she always finishes homework at school.
Again, a call to the teacher will provide the answer. If you find that this is true—that assignments are completed at school—you may want to encourage your child to set aside some time each night just for reading, a great habit to get into.

Before you talk to your child's teacher, write down any questions you may have. Here are some questions you may wish to address:

- Is homework given every single night?
- How long should my child be spending on homework each night?
- What should I do if my child does not understand how to do the work?
- How much should I help my child?
- Should I have my child correct mistakes?
- How much does homework count toward my child's total grade?

By working with the teacher you will show your child that you care about homework being done every single day, and that you and the teacher are joining together to help him or her succeed.

Tips for Contacting the Teacher

Don't put the teacher on the defensive. Instead, open the conversation by talking about your concern for your child. For example:

"I'm concerned that my child doesn't understand the assignment. Can you work with me to solve this problem?"

"I'm concerned that my child waits until the last minute to do projects. Can we work together so that I know ahead of time what the schedule will be for long-range assignments?"

If Homework Problems Persist . . .

✔ You've established Daily Homework Time.

✔ You've set up a study area for your child and put together a Homework Survival Kit.

✔ You've explained why homework is important.

✔ You've taken specific steps to solve ongoing homework problems.

✔ You've given plenty of praise.

✔ You've talked to the teacher.

But your child is still having problems doing homework. It's time to back up your words with stronger actions. It's time to use a Homework Contract.

What is a Homework Contract?

This contract is a written agreement between you and your child that states:

1) The specific homework rule that must be followed.
2) The specific reward your child will receive for following the homework rule.
3) The privileges that will be taken away if your child doesn't do his or her homework appropriately.

Rules

Meet with your child to talk about the specific problem he or she is having with homework. Explain that homework is too important to be avoided or done badly. Depending on your child's problem, the homework rule may be:

___ Homework will be brought home from school each day.

___ Homework will be completed each night during Daily Homework Time.

___ Homework will be done neatly.

___ Homework will be done on your own to the best of your ability.

__ Other ______________________

Say to your child, for example:

"Barry, homework is too important to let slide like this, so let me explain what we're going to do. First of all, we're going to have a new rule about homework. The new rule is this: Homework will be completed each night during Daily Homework Time. No excuses. No exceptions. And since Daily Homework Time is right after school I will expect to see all homework done by dinner time."

Write the new rule on the Homework Contract (pages 45-46).

Rewards

The goal is for your child to be successful with the new rule, and to get his or her homework done. In order to do so, offer your child an incentive. For example, each night your child chooses to follow the rule he or she may:

___ Have a friend over on the weekend.

___ Earn extra "stay up" time on the weekend.

___ Watch a favorite "before bed" video with Mom or Dad.

___ Earn extra story-reading time with Mom or Dad.

___ Earn five minutes of music in bed.

___ Other ______________________

Say to you child, for example:

"I believe you can stick to this rule and when you do I want to let you know that I appreciate it. How does this sound? Every night that your homework is completed during Daily Homework Time I'll add a check mark to this chart. If you get check marks Monday through Thursday then you can invite a friend to sleep over on Friday."

Write the reward on the Homework Contract (pages 45-46).

Consequences

Decide what privilege or activity you will *take away* if your child does not follow the new rule. For example, your child might:

___ Lose the privilege of playing with friends after school.

___ Lose telephone privileges.

___ Have to go to his or her bedroom earlier.

___ Lose radio, stereo or TV privileges.

___ Other ______________________

Say to your child, for example:

"Barry, if you don't choose to follow the rule and your homework is not completed during Daily Homework Time, you will lose all TV and telephone privileges during the week. Homework is important and unless you complete it responsibly there will be no phone and no TV."

Write the consequence on the Homework Contract (pages 45-46).

Sign it and date it.

Once the contract is completed, sign and date it. Then post it on a cupboard, bulletin board or the refrigerator door.

HOMEWORK
CONTRACT

The new rule in our house will be:

Complete homework during D.H.T.
New Rule

If *Barry*
Child's Name

does follow the rule,

he gets one check mark on the Homework Tracker.
Reward

If *Barry*
Child's Name

does not follow the rule,

he will lose TV and phone privileges during that week.
Consequence

Parent's Signature

Child's Signature

Date

Remember, you must be consistent.

- If your child breaks the rule, you must follow through with the consequence.
- If your child follows the rule, you must provide the reward.
- Praise your child whenever he or she follows the rule.

How to Speak So Your Child Will Listen

She doesn't listen to a thing I say!

Does your child tune you out, ignore you, or argue with you when you ask him or her to do homework (or anything else, for that matter)? If this is typical in your home it may have a lot to do with the way *you* are speaking to your child.

Parents who are successful in encouraging better behavior speak to their children in a clear, direct and firm manner that leaves no doubt about what is expected.

Parents who are ignored or argued with often speak in a way that is either wishy washy or hostile.

Do any of these comments sound familiar?

"How many times do I have to remind you to start your homework?"

"Please won't you get going on your homework? It's getting late."

"This report is due tomorrow and you've barely begun."

"Why can't you bring the books you need home with you?"

Chances are you've said things like these many times. Most parents have. But what do statements like these really say to your child? Look at each one carefully and you will see that they either ask pointless questions, beg, or make an obvious statement of fact. In the examples above, none of those all-too-common statements are likely to motivate a child to jump up and get to work. Wishy-washy statements don't let your child know that your words are to be taken seriously—that you mean business.

They make it easy for your child to ignore you.

And what about comments like these?

"I should know better than to expect you to get your homework done on time."

"I've had it with getting calls from your teacher. If you miss one more assignment you're really going to get it."

"That's it. You're grounded for two weeks."

What do these all-too-common remarks say to a child? Put-downs, meaningless threats and off-the-wall punishments, because they are emotional and often inappropriate, are an invitation to challenge and anger. Because they disregard a child's feelings they send a message to the child that says, "I don't like you." Hostile responses are ultimately damaging. The words your child hears from you will become the way he or she feels about himself or herself.

Learn to speak so your child will listen.

Don't beg. Don't get angry. Don't become exasperated. Instead, when making a request of your child, be calm and use direct statements that send your child this message: "This is what I expect you to do."

"Lisa, go to your study area and begin your homework now."

"Howard, I expect you to complete all your homework during Daily Homework Time."

"Nancy, I want you to rewrite this page neatly so that I can read it."

Confident, clear and direct statements get results.

And if your child argues?

Above all, don't argue back. Do not get involved in a discussion. It will get you nowhere. The following scene illustrates this point:

Parent: (*to daughter on telephone*) Lisa, it's seven o'clock. Time to begin homework.

Child: Ok, ok. In a few minutes. I've just got to finish telling Mandy something important.

Parent: I'm sure whatever it is can wait. You've already talked to Mandy three times tonight.

Child: I have not. Amanda's been on the phone, not me.

Parent: Lisa, that phone's been glued to your ear for over an hour. Don't you think homework is a little more important than talking to Mandy about boys?

Child: We're not talking about boys. If you just let me finish I'll get to my homework in a few minutes.

Parent: You say a few minutes and it ends up an hour. . .

What happened here? By arguing—by getting into a pointless discussion—the parent has lost control of the situation. Lisa is still on the phone. Homework is not getting done. And the parent is angry and frustrated. What should you do in a situation like this?

Don't argue. Use the "broken record" technique.

First, very clearly tell your child what you want her to do. If she argues, simply repeat the statement, like a broken record. Do not argue back or even discuss the issue. *Repeat your expectation.*

For example:

Parent: (*to daughter on telephone*) Lisa, I want you to hang up the phone and begin your homework now.

Child: Ok, ok. In a few minutes. I've just got to finish telling Mandy something important.

Parent: I understand you want to talk to Mandy, but Daily Homework Time starts now. Hang up the phone and get to work.

Child: That's not fair. Mandy was absent today and I've got to tell her some stuff.

Parent: I understand that Lisa, but I want you to hang up and begin your homework now. You can call her back when you've finished your homework.

By staying firm, not arguing, not getting sidetracked, chances are good your child will comply with your request. He or she may grumble and complain, but will probably get up and take care of the job.

If necessary, back up your words with actions.

If, however, after three repetitions of your expectations your child still does not comply, it's time to back up your words with actions and present your child with a clear choice:

Parent: Lisa, I expect you to begin your homework now. If you choose not to begin your homework you will choose to lose phone privileges the next 2 days. The choice is yours.

By giving your child a choice you place responsibility for what happens right where it belongs—squarely on your child's shoulders.

Try these techniques the next time your child balks at fulfilling a responsibility or responding to a request. Just take a deep breath and follow through calmly and confidently. You'll find that this approach *does* work!

Pages 35 - 46 contain the Homework Worksheets that were introduced in this book. Two copies of most worksheets were provided. You may want to make additional copies before using so there will always be an ample supply on hand.

LONG-RANGE PLANNER

Name ______________________ Date __________

Assignment ______________________ Due Date __________

STEP 1 ______________________ Date to be Completed __________

STEP 2 ______________________ Date to be Completed __________

STEP 3 ______________________ Date to be Completed __________

STEP 4 ______________________ Date to be Completed __________

STEP 5 ______________________ Date to be Completed __________

STEP 6 ______________________ Date to be Completed __________

STEP 7 ______________________ Date to be Completed __________

STEP 8 ______________________ Date to be Completed __________

LONG-RANGE PLANNER

Name ______________________ Date __________

Assignment ______________________ Due Date __________

STEP 1	______________________ ______________________	Date to be Completed __________
STEP 2	______________________ ______________________	Date to be Completed __________
STEP 3	______________________ ______________________	Date to be Completed __________
STEP 4	______________________ ______________________	Date to be Completed __________
STEP 5	______________________ ______________________	Date to be Completed __________
STEP 6	______________________ ______________________	Date to be Completed __________
STEP 7	______________________ ______________________	Date to be Completed __________
STEP 8	______________________ ______________________	Date to be Completed __________

Do Not Disturb!

Homework is FUN

After it's done!

Daily SCHEDULE

MONDAY Homework Time: ______________ to ______________

3:00 PM		7:00 PM	
4:00 PM		8:00 PM	
5:00 PM		9:00 PM	
6:00 PM		10:00 PM	

TUESDAY Homework Time: ______________ to ______________

3:00 PM		7:00 PM	
4:00 PM		8:00 PM	
5:00 PM		9:00 PM	
6:00 PM		10:00 PM	

WEDNESDAY Homework Time: ______________ to ______________

3:00 PM		7:00 PM	
4:00 PM		8:00 PM	
5:00 PM		9:00 PM	
6:00 PM		10:00 PM	

THURSDAY Homework Time: ______________ to ______________

3:00 PM		7:00 PM	
4:00 PM		8:00 PM	
5:00 PM		9:00 PM	
6:00 PM		10:00 PM	

FRIDAY Homework Time: ______________ to ______________

3:00 PM		7:00 PM	
4:00 PM		8:00 PM	
5:00 PM		9:00 PM	
6:00 PM		10:00 PM	

Daily SCHEDULE

MONDAY Homework Time:______________ to ______________

3:00 PM	______________	7:00 PM	______________
4:00 PM	______________	8:00 PM	______________
5:00 PM	______________	9:00 PM	______________
6:00 PM	______________	10:00 PM	______________

TUESDAY Homework Time:______________ to ______________

3:00 PM	______________	7:00 PM	______________
4:00 PM	______________	8:00 PM	______________
5:00 PM	______________	9:00 PM	______________
6:00 PM	______________	10:00 PM	______________

WEDNESDAY Homework Time:______________ to ______________

3:00 PM	______________	7:00 PM	______________
4:00 PM	______________	8:00 PM	______________
5:00 PM	______________	9:00 PM	______________
6:00 PM	______________	10:00 PM	______________

THURSDAY Homework Time:______________ to ______________

3:00 PM	______________	7:00 PM	______________
4:00 PM	______________	8:00 PM	______________
5:00 PM	______________	9:00 PM	______________
6:00 PM	______________	10:00 PM	______________

FRIDAY Homework Time:______________ to ______________

3:00 PM	______________	7:00 PM	______________
4:00 PM	______________	8:00 PM	______________
5:00 PM	______________	9:00 PM	______________
6:00 PM	______________	10:00 PM	______________

Homework TRACKER

Week of:	Monday	Tuesday	Wednesday	Thursday	Friday
____ to ____					
____ to ____					
____ to ____					
____ to ____					

Use this sheet to keep track of completed homework. Check off one square each night that all homework is completed.

Homework TRACKER

Week of:	Monday	Tuesday	Wednesday	Thursday	Friday
____ to ____					
____ to ____					
____ to ____					
____ to ____					

Use this sheet to keep track of completed homework. Check off one square each night that all homework is completed.

Homework TRACKER

Week of:	Monday	Tuesday	Wednesday	Thursday	Friday
____ to ____					
____ to ____					
____ to ____					
____ to ____					

Use this sheet to keep track of completed homework. Check off one square each night that all homework is completed.

Homework TRACKER

Week of:	Monday	Tuesday	Wednesday	Thursday	Friday
____ to ____					
____ to ____					
____ to ____					
____ to ____					

Use this sheet to keep track of completed homework. Check off one square each night that all homework is completed.

Homework
Coupon

NEAT
&
COMPLETE

Your work looks great this week! Let's celebrate with lunch on ____________

HOMEWORK COUPON

Outstanding Planning!

Here's something special just for you! ____________

HOMEWORK COUPON

HOMEWORK Super

This coupon entitles you to

____

____

____

____

HOMEWORK COUPON

Great Job!

____

____

____

HOMEWORK COUPON

NEAT & COMPLETE

Your work looks great this week! Let's celebrate with lunch on ________

HOMEWORK COUPON

Outstanding Planning!

Here's something special just for you! ________

HOMEWORK COUPON

HOMEWORK Super

This coupon entitles you to

____

____

____

____

HOMEWORK COUPON

Great Job!

____

____

____

HOMEWORK COUPON

HOMEWORK CONTRACT

The new rule in our house will be:

New Rule

If

Child's Name

does follow the rule,

Reward

If

Child's Name

does not follow the rule,

Consequence

Parent's Signature

Child's Signature

Date

HOMEWORK CONTRACT

The new rule in our house will be:

____
New Rule

If ______________________________
Child's Name

does follow the rule,

____
Reward

____

If ______________________________
Child's Name

does not follow the rule,

____
Consequence

____

____
Parent's Signature

____
Child's Signature

____
Date

Lee Canter's

Top 10 Homework Reminders

As long as your child is in school, homework will continue to be a fact of life. With a little planning, it can be a successful fact of life. You've taken the first steps by following the plan presented in this book. Here then are our Top Ten Homework Reminders to help you keep things on track and running smoothly. Refer to these reminders from time to time whenever you need a quick refresher!

1 Most of your child's important activities (sports practice, doctor visits and music lessons) are scheduled. Homework should be too. With your child decide on an appropriate time that homework will be done each night. Encourage your child to begin and complete homework during this daily homework time.

2 Your child may think he or she can study with the TV on and family members all around, but experts agree that a quiet study environment is a must for a child to do his or her best work. Make sure your child has a quiet place to study at a desk or table, and insist that all homework is done there. It's important to maintain these expectations as your child grows older.

3 It's tough for children to do homework successfully when they run out of critical supplies like paper, pencils, markers, ruler, folders, glue and index cards. A Homework Survival Kit that contains these and other homework basics will be a real lifesaver for you and your child.

4 Tired of frustrating morning hunts for missing homework assignments? A Homework Drop Spot can solve this problem. Choose a place where your child puts all completed assignments the night before. In the morning all he or she has to do is stop by and pick them up.

5 Your consistent message to your child about homework should be: "Homework is important to your success in school and I expect homework to be done appropriately." It is critical that your child understands that you place as much importance on homework being done each night as you do your child going to school each day. The attitude you project will go a long way toward communicating your expectations.

6 No doubt your child would rather be doing many things other than homework. All the more reason to be generous with your praise. Let your child know how proud you are of the hard work he or she is doing. Check assignments and offer well-deserved praise for the efforts he or she makes. Your praise, more than anything else, will motivate your child to keep up the good work.

7 Don't hesitate to call your child's teacher if you have any concerns at all about homework (or any other school-related issues). Very often the teacher can suggest a solution to a problem that might be bothering you or your child.

8 Take a genuine interest in homework assignments. Your child works hard at homework and deserves more than a perfunctory "that's nice." When your child shows you his or her work really look at it, ask questions and offer specific comments: "What a beautiful poem. I can feel the ocean winds as I read." "This is an excellent map you've drawn. The proportions are right on." "You really had to think carefully to do these math problems. Great job!"

9 In spite of everything you do, some homework problems just aren't solved easily. Keep in mind that it's to your benefit, and your child's, to actively help him or her acquire appropriate homework habits. A homework contract (as described in this book) will give you the structure you sometimes need to get your child on track.

10 Check your child's list of assignments each night to make sure all homework is getting done, to stay involved with what's going on in class, to answer any questions your child may have, and to alert yourself to any upcoming long-range assignments and tests. This is the best tool you have for staying involved and informed. Provide your child with an assignment book if necessary and insist that all homework assignments are written down.